INVERARAY
CASTLE

ANCESTRAL HOME OF THE DUKES OF ARGYLL

Designed, edited & photographed by Nick McCann
Published by Heritage House Group

My family and I welcome you to Inveraray Castle.

Today, the childish exuberance of the next generation continues to keep the castle alive. Just as I grew up here, it is now home to my young family. For our many visitors from around the world, we try to emphasise that it is not a museum - although there is plenty to see - but a family home. We take great pride in the friendly atmosphere we have tried to create and hope that you will take full advantage of the opportunities we have provided.

Our team of knowledgeable guides is here to help you understand and enjoy the castle, the history, the wonderful furniture and objets d'art, as well as anecdotes about the family past and present, even the paranormal ancestors. The Dukes of Argyll and the Campbells have played a major part in the rich history of the West Coast of Scotland, as well as being prominent players in the development of Great Britain.

The gardens have been recently opened to everyone and they highlight the temperate climate we enjoy thanks to the Gulf Stream. The rhododendrons and azaleas in May and June are the envy of many a gardener and for me it is one of the most beautiful times to be here.

We are very fortunate to have wonderful local produce in Argyll and my wife showcases some of our family favourites in the tearoom: wonderful local smoked salmon, cheese, ham, ice-cream and freshly baked cakes (or a Duke's Special hot chocolate), all there to add the finishing touch to your visit. In the gift shop my mother has personally chosen a range of items for you to browse through: choose a lasting memento of Inveraray, a gift to take home, or sample a West Coast whisky from one of the famous distilleries.

You can keep up to date with developments at the castle through our website, where you can also arrange a wedding, a dinner, an exclusive corporate or sporting event, or book a holiday in one of our range of holiday cottages or parks.

www.inveraray-castle.com

We hope that you enjoy your visit and look forward to welcoming you back to Inveraray.

NE OBLIVISCARIS

Foreword from the Duke of Argyll

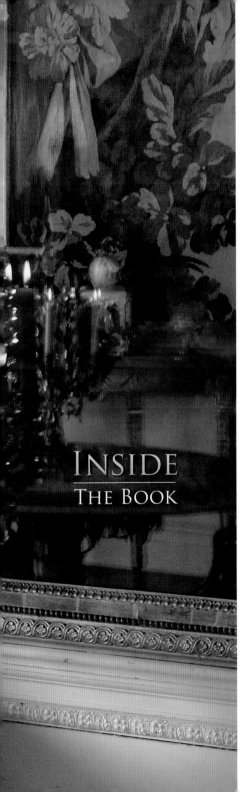

INSIDE
THE BOOK

The Campbell Family
Earls & Dukes of Argyll

THE CAMPBELL KNIGHTS OF LOCHOW

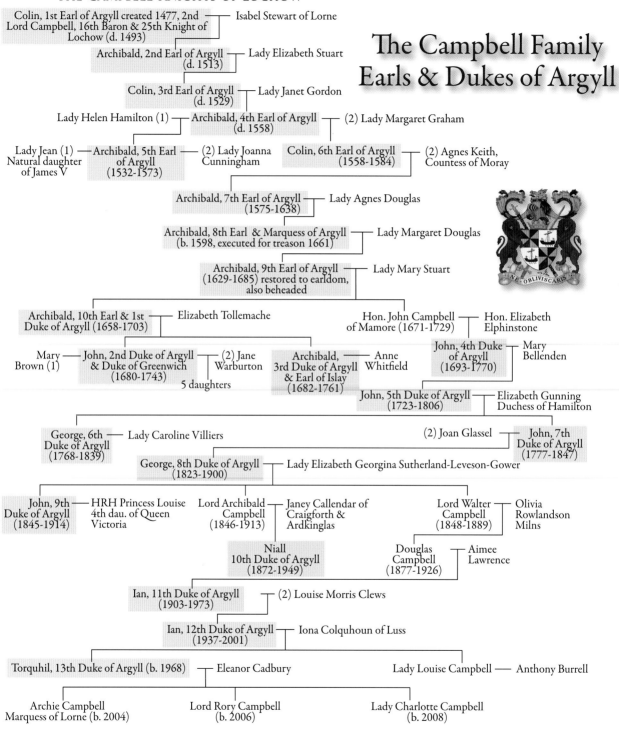

Colin, 1st Earl of Argyll created 1477, 2nd Lord Campbell, 16th Baron & 25th Knight of Lochow (d. 1493) — Isabel Stewart of Lorne

Archibald, 2nd Earl of Argyll (d. 1513) — Lady Elizabeth Stuart

Colin, 3rd Earl of Argyll (d. 1529) — Lady Janet Gordon

Lady Helen Hamilton (1) — Archibald, 4th Earl of Argyll (d. 1558) — (2) Lady Margaret Graham

Lady Jean (1) Natural daughter of James V — Archibald, 5th Earl of Argyll (1532-1573) — (2) Lady Joanna Cunningham

Colin, 6th Earl of Argyll (1558-1584) — (2) Agnes Keith, Countess of Moray

Archibald, 7th Earl of Argyll (1575-1638) — Lady Agnes Douglas

Archibald, 8th Earl & Marquess of Argyll (b. 1598, executed for treason 1661) — Lady Margaret Douglas

Archibald, 9th Earl of Argyll (1629-1685) restored to earldom, also beheaded — Lady Mary Stuart

Archibald, 10th Earl & 1st Duke of Argyll (1658-1703) — Elizabeth Tollemache

Hon. John Campbell of Mamore (1671-1729) — Hon. Elizabeth Elphinstone

Mary Brown (1) — John, 2nd Duke of Argyll & Duke of Greenwich (1680-1743) — (2) Jane Warburton — 5 daughters

Archibald, 3rd Duke of Argyll & Earl of Islay (1682-1761) — Anne Whitfield

John, 4th Duke of Argyll (1693-1770) — Mary Bellenden

John, 5th Duke of Argyll (1723-1806) — Elizabeth Gunning Duchess of Hamilton

George, 6th Duke of Argyll (1768-1839) — Lady Caroline Villiers

(2) Joan Glassel — John, 7th Duke of Argyll (1777-1847)

George, 8th Duke of Argyll (1823-1900) — Lady Elizabeth Georgina Sutherland-Leveson-Gower

John, 9th Duke of Argyll (1845-1914) — HRH Princess Louise 4th dau. of Queen Victoria

Lord Archibald Campbell (1846-1913) — Janey Callendar of Craigforth & Ardkinglas

Lord Walter Campbell (1848-1889) — Olivia Rowlandson Milns

Niall 10th Duke of Argyll (1872-1949)

Douglas Campbell (1877-1926) — Aimee Lawrence

Ian, 11th Duke of Argyll (1903-1973) — (2) Louise Morris Clews

Ian, 12th Duke of Argyll (1937-2001) — Iona Colquhoun of Luss

Torquhil, 13th Duke of Argyll (b. 1968) — Eleanor Cadbury

Lady Louise Campbell — Anthony Burrell

Archie Campbell Marquess of Lorne (b. 2004)

Lord Rory Campbell (b. 2006)

Lady Charlotte Campbell (b. 2008)

NE OBLIVISCARIS

LINEAGE

THE CAMPBELL FAMILY - EARLS & DUKES OF ARGYLL

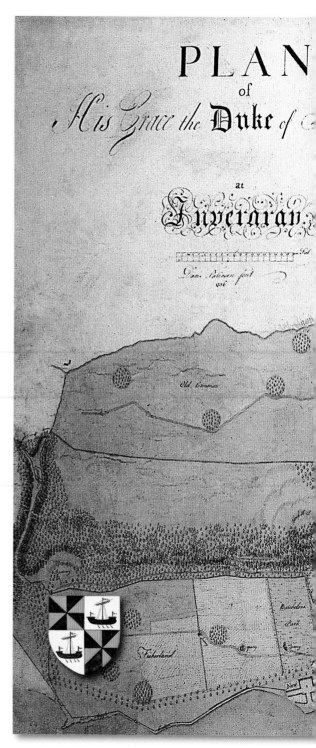

The Campbells, thought to be of British stock from the Kingdom of Strathclyde, probably arrived in Argyll as part of a royal expedition in *c.*1220. They settled on Lochaweside where they were placed in charge of the king's lands in the area.

The Chief of Clan Campbell takes his Gaelic title of '*MacCailein Mor*' from Colin Mor Campbell - '*Colin the Great*' who was killed in a quarrel with the MacDougalls of Lorne in 1296. His son was Sir Neil Campbell, boon companion and brother-in-law of King Robert the Bruce, whose son, Sir Colin, was rewarded in 1315 by the grant of the lands of Lochawe and Ardscotnish of which he now became the Lord. Although at this stage, the Campbells of Lochawe were not without rivals for the leadership of the emerging Clan Campbell, they were soon the pre-eminent family and acknowledged as such as they extended their power and landholdings.

moved headquarters to Inveraray

From Bruce's time at least, their headquarters had been at the great castle of Innischonnell, on Loch Awe. Around the mid 1400s, Sir Duncan Campbell of Lochawe, great grandson of Sir Colin, moved his headquarters to Inveraray, commanding most of the landward communications of Argyll, well placed for control of the new Campbell lands in Cowal and with convenient saltwater connections. In 1445 he was created Lord Campbell, and thereafter, a steady string of titles became attached to members of the family. His grandson Colin was created Earl of Argyll in 1457; he married one of the three daughters of the last Stewart Lord of Lorne and by a deal with his wife's uncle obtained that lordship for himself in 1470. Thereafter the Campbell Chiefs quartered the Galley of Lorne in their arms (right). Archibald, the 2nd Earl fell with his King at Flodden in 1513; he was the first of the family to hold the appointment of Master of the Royal Household in Scotland, still held by the Duke today. The 5th Earl commanded a force of his own people which exceeded in strength the existing armies of France and England; he was a power of international importance but his star was extinguished by his defeat when in command of the army of Mary Queen of Scots at Langside in 1568.

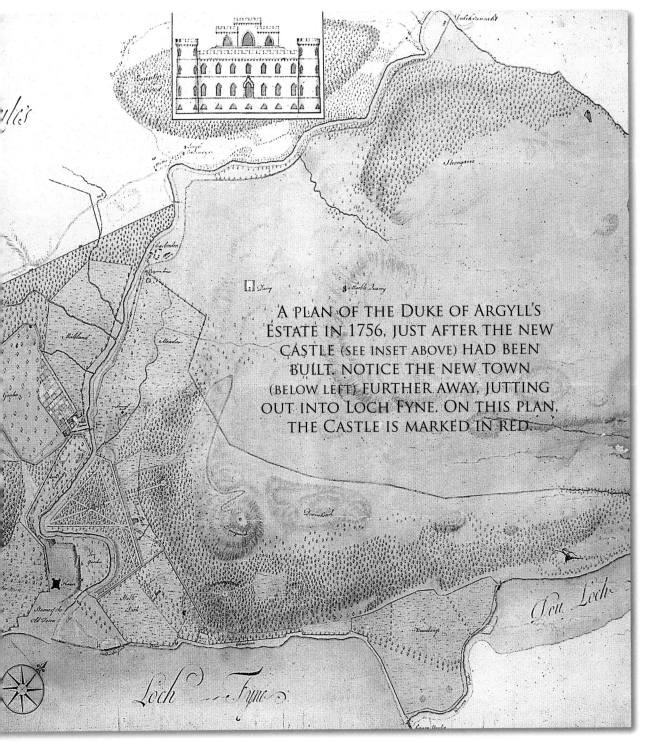

A PLAN OF THE DUKE OF ARGYLL'S ESTATE IN 1756, JUST AFTER THE NEW CASTLE (SEE INSET ABOVE) HAD BEEN BUILT. NOTICE THE NEW TOWN (BELOW LEFT) FURTHER AWAY, JUTTING OUT INTO LOCH FYNE. ON THIS PLAN, THE CASTLE IS MARKED IN RED.

Inveraray Castle - The Campbells

a bitter and ruthless character

The 7th Earl was known as '*Gillespie Gruamach*' - '*Grim-faced Archie*' - no wonder since in his youth a gang of plotting Campbells sought to take his life and that of his younger brother. He survived but was a bitter and ruthless character whose ferocity against the MacGregors was legendary. He eventually quitted the Highlands leaving the area in disarray without his leadership and went abroad, converting to Roman Catholicism at the behest of his wife.

slaughtered and destroyed

His son, also Archibald, the 8th Earl and later Marquess of Argyll, was arguably the greatest and certainly the most misunderstood Campbell Chief. His devotion to the Presbyterian religion led him reluctantly into enmity with King Charles I whose Lieutenant General, Montrose, invaded Inveraray unexpectedly at New Year 1645. The Royalists killed and ravaged mercilessly before withdrawing to the north. By a countermarch through the mountains, they surprised the Campbell forces at Inverlochy and again imposed a crushing defeat on them. The Marquess who had only just escaped from Inveraray again had to flee for his life, an unfortunate record whose burden he had to bear for the rest of his days. Later that year, Montrose's second-in-command, Alasdair Mac Colla, invaded Argyll once again with his Irish MacDonalds and for several months slaughtered and destroyed all that came in his path before the Covenanter forces eventually prevailed. At the Restoration, Argyll hastened to London but instead of gratitude, he was thrown into the Tower before being returned to Scotland for trial and execution, a fate that he faced with courage.

captured and summarily executed

The fortunes of the House of Argyll were restored by the 9th Earl, who, unlike his father did not receive the rank of Marquess. He was out of sympathy with the religious moves of King James VII and invaded Scotland in 1685 at the same time that the Duke of Monmouth landed in the South. Both were unsuccessful and Argyll, fleeing to the lowlands, was captured and summarily executed. The Glorious Revolution of 1688 brought a change in the climate of the country and the 10th Earl was very much in favour, being granted a Dukedom in 1701 together with a string of subsidiary titles. Before that however, in 1689, he had raised a Regiment for the Crown, The Earl of Argyle's Regiment of Foot. This was the unit tasked with carrying out the notorious Massacre of Glencoe in 1692, an episode usually thereafter inaccurately classed as an act of clan vengeance by the Campbells. In fact it was a deliberate act of government policy carried out under orders which had been signed by the King himself by a unit of the regular British Army.

7th Earl | 9th Earl
1st Duke | 2nd
3rd | 4th
5th | 6th
7th | 8th

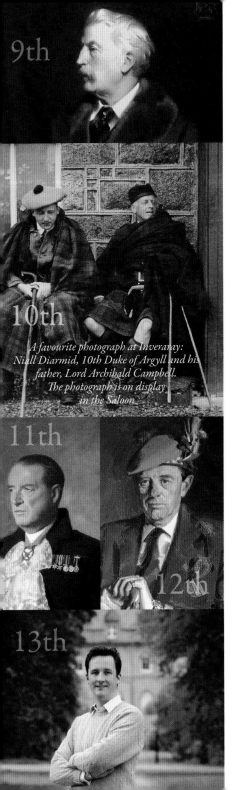

9th

10th

*A favourite photograph at Inveraray:
Niall Diarmid, 10th Duke of Argyll and his
father, Lord Archibald Campbell.
The photograph is on display
in the Saloon*

11th

12th

13th

promoted to Field Marshal

The 2nd Duke was a famous soldier who has been favourably compared with his contemporary rival Marlborough. He commanded the Government Army at the Battle of Sheriffmuir which put paid to the Jacobite Rebellion of 1715 and was one of the first two officers in the British Army to be promoted to the rank of Field Marshal. He was created Duke of Greenwich in 1719 but the title lapsed on his death without a male heir when the Dukedom of Argyll passed to his younger brother Archibald as 3rd Duke. Archibald had already been raised to the Peerage as Earl of Ilay; another distinguished soldier, he left the Army for politics, becoming Lord Justice General of Scotland.

a charming but dissolute playboy

He, too, died without a male heir and the Dukedom now passed to his cousin John, 4th Duke of Argyll, another soldier of renown who reached the rank of full General. His son, John the 5th Duke, carried on the tradition, being the second member of the family to attain the rank of Field Marshal. His far-seeing efforts to improve the estate were almost destroyed by his elder son the 6th Duke, a charming but dissolute playboy who left a string of debts and illegitimate children. His brother, the 7th Duke fought hard to avoid complete disaster to the family fortunes which were to an extent restored by the time of the succession of the 8th Duke who was a successful politician, a Cabinet Minister and Renaissance Man of considerable stature, and author of a string of scientific and scholarly works. It was his son and heir, the Marquess of Lorne who married Queen Victoria's daughter, Princess Louise, thereafter serving as Governor-General of Canada before succeeding as 9th Duke.

a gallant officer

They had no children and the title went to a nephew, Niall, 10th Duke, something of a scholarly recluse in later life with the history of his family and clan his major interest. He never married and on his death in 1949, the title passed to his cousin, Ian, the 11th Duke. A gallant officer taken prisoner with most of the Highland Division in France in 1940, his predilection for cafe society recalled somewhat his predecessor the 6th Duke. He was succeeded in 1973 by his elder son, Ian, the 12th Duke, who laboured hard to restore the Argyll name, becoming in due course Lord Lieutenant of Argyll and Bute as well as meticulously carrying out the traditional duties of the family's head.

MacCailein Mor

He died in 2001 and has been succeeded by his son Torquhil who became the 13th Duke of Argyll and MacCailein Mor; in June 2002 he married Miss Eleanor Cadbury. They have three children and live in the Castle today.

CLOSE TO THE EAST SHORE OF NEARBY LOCH AWE, IS A SMALL ISLAND.
IN WINTER, THROUGH THE TREES, IT IS POSSIBLE TO GLIMPSE THE HIGH WALLS
OF A RUINED STRONGHOLD. THIS IS INNISCHONNELL CASTLE - THE ORIGINAL
HOME OF THE CAMPBELL CHIEFS. BY THE END OF THE 15TH CENTURY
IT HAD BEEN ADANDONED AND THE CAMPBELLS HAD RELOCATED TO
INVERARAY ON THE SHORES OF LOCH FYNE.

GRAND
DESIGNS

THE DEVELOPMENT OF
THE CASTLE

*For a more detailed history of the building of Inveraray
Castle, see 'Inveraray and the Dukes of Argyll'
by Ian G. Lindsay and Mary Cosh
(Edinburgh University Press 1973)*

*This Victorian 'baronial'
addition by Anthony Salvin
for the 8th Duke in the 1870s,
was never built, but the conical
roofs on the corner towers were
adopted giving Inveraray
a finished look it
did not have before*

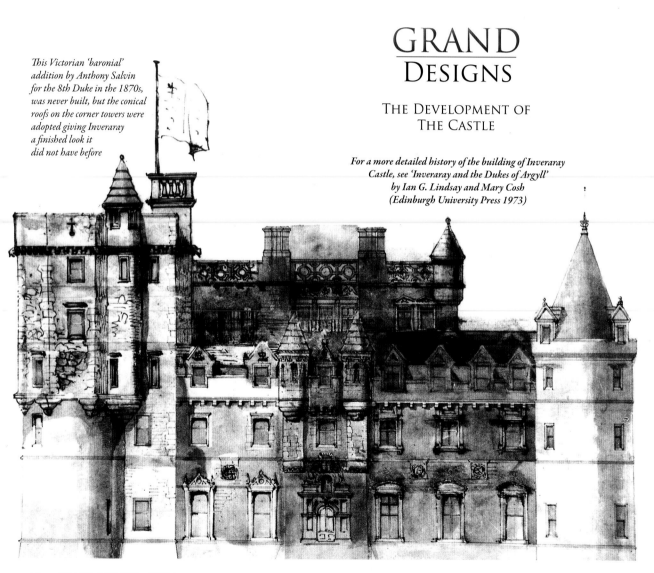

Close up detail from Thomas Sandby's drawing of 1746, clearly showing the laird's tower and huddle of simple dwellings

For two centuries all that existed was a rudimentary laird's tower and a few houses huddled together within sight of it. The 1st Earl of Argyll (died 1493), founded the burgh of Inveraray and began the very long process of opening up this part of the west coast of Scotland, but it wasn't until eight generations later that work began on the great house we see today.

John, the 2nd Duke of Argyll (1680-1743), asked Sir John Vanbrugh, the playwright, and architect of Blenheim Palace and Castle Howard, to design something befitting the family's elevation to the Dukedom. Vanbrugh came up with an idea for a fairly simple building of one storey, four-square around a courtyard and incorporating four corner towers, each with a conical cap. Although this came to nothing and Vanbrugh was dead within six years, the great architect's germ of an idea became the base of the house which the 2nd Duke's brother, Duke Archibald (1682-1761), was eventually to build.

When Duke Archibald succeeded, the little town was so remote, visitors needed guides to navigate primitive tracks over heather and mountain. The most sensible, in fact the only real way, to reach Inveraray at that time was by ship or boat and in the 1750s, as the Castle was slowly taking shape, the quayside of Inveraray was crowded with vessels bearing lead, iron, timber, glass, slates and other building material, not only for the Castle, but also for the re-building of the town itself.

The foundation stone of the Castle was laid in 1746 and what followed was the construction - to a design by the architect Roger Morris - of a truly modern, baroque, Palladian and Gothic-style castle, architecturally before its time.

Building the Castle was a slow process, so that even when Dr Johnson and Boswell visited the 5th Duke in 1773, on their famous tour of Scotland, the Duke had only been in residence for about three years and work was not to be completed until 1789, a full 43 years after the foundation stone was laid!

The Castle in 1810; apart from the conical tower roofs, remarkably similar in appearance to today

A dark and brooding image of the new Castle with the ruins of the old laird's tower and town around 1760

South front of the Castle before the fire of 1877

South Front
of
INVERARY CASTLE

A further unexecuted design for a more 'baronial' Castle by Salvin in the 1870s

The Castle you see today is the result of two fires. The first, on October 12th 1877, did extensive damage and the 8th Duke and his family took themselves off to their other house at Rosneath, near Helensburgh, while restoration took place. The architect Anthony Salvin was employed to repair and improve the damaged building. Although his designs for a Victorian 'baronial' wing were not taken up, he was responsible for the conical roofs on the corner towers, so familiar to visitors today.

AFTER WORLD WAR II, THE 11TH DUKE OF ARGYLL & DUCHESS MARGARET UNDERTOOK A MAJOR PROGRAMME OF REPAIR AND RENOVATION AND OPENED THE CASTLE TO THE PUBLIC IN THE CORONATION YEAR, 1953

The second fire, in 1975, ravaged the top storey of the Castle destroying pictures and furniture stored there. The vast torrents of water from the fire hoses cascaded through the State Rooms damaging the decoration. The people of the town provided invaluable assistance in salvaging furniture and works of art, and the young 12th Duke was faced with the daunting task of restoring his ancestral home. Thanks to the Duke & Duchess's determination and to the efforts of many others, the restored Inveraray Castle is today one of Scotland's greatest treasures.

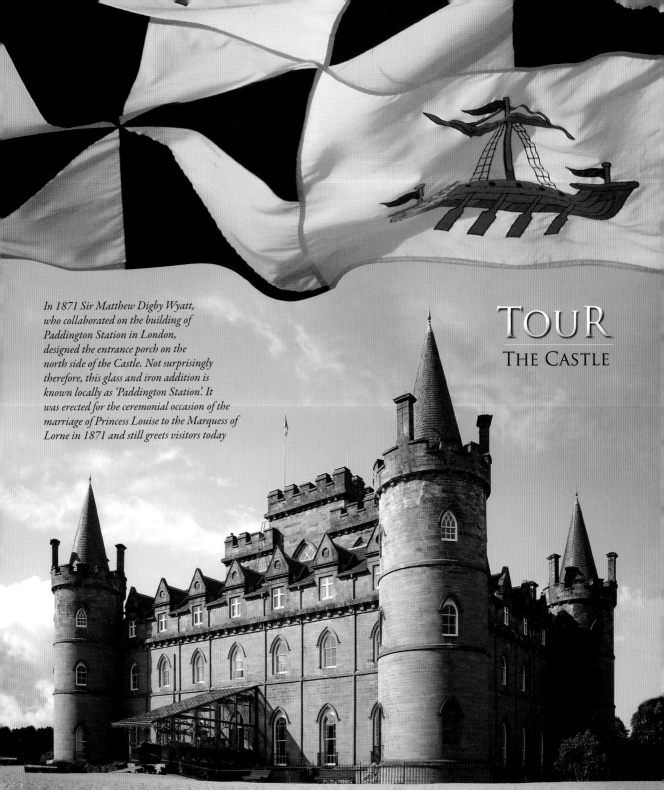

In 1871 Sir Matthew Digby Wyatt, who collaborated on the building of Paddington Station in London, designed the entrance porch on the north side of the Castle. Not surprisingly therefore, this glass and iron addition is known locally as 'Paddington Station'. It was erected for the ceremonial occasion of the marriage of Princess Louise to the Marquess of Lorne in 1871 and still greets visitors today

TOUR
THE CASTLE

TO THE LEFT IS THE STATE DINING ROOM   TO THE RIGHT, THE TAPESTRY DRAWING ROOM
AND STRAIGHT AHEAD, THE ARMOURY HALL

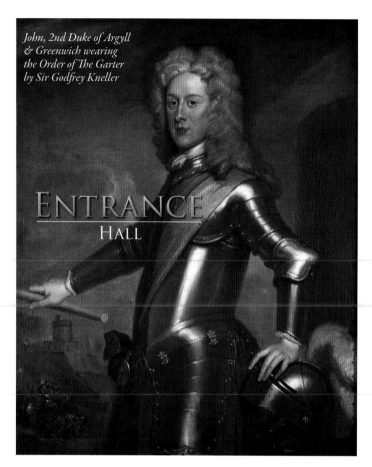

John, 2nd Duke of Argyll & Greenwich wearing the Order of The Garter by Sir Godfrey Kneller

ENTRANCE
HALL

John, 7th Duke of Argyll in ermine robes

The cannon balls were recovered from Tobermory Bay on the Isle of Mull

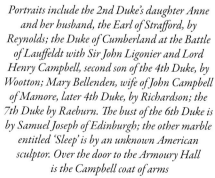

The modest scale of the Entrance Hall may come as a surprise but it arose from a change of mind by the 5th Duke in 1772. Originally the castle was to be entered from the south side but it was then decided to move the entrance to the north side and to divide the original long gallery to form a large drawing and dining room either side of a small hall. This seems to have been arranged around the end of the 18th century in 1772, but the decoration of the hall with its delicate Gothic plasterwork was not designed until 1780.

Portraits include the 2nd Duke's daughter Anne and her husband, the Earl of Strafford, by Reynolds; the Duke of Cumberland at the Battle of Lauffeldt with Sir John Ligonier and Lord Henry Campbell, second son of the 4th Duke, by Wootton; Mary Bellenden, wife of John Campbell of Mamore, later 4th Duke, by Richardson; the 7th Duke by Raeburn. The bust of the 6th Duke is by Samuel Joseph of Edinburgh; the other marble entitled 'Sleep' is by an unknown American sculptor. Over the door to the Armoury Hall is the Campbell coat of arms

Grisaille roundel of 'Autumn'
- one of a set of four - naturally, of The Seasons

To the right, painted panels by Girard & Guinand

The 3rd Duke had not set aside a room specially for eating in, but by 1770 fashions had changed and such a room was essential. That was, no doubt, part of the reason for the 5th Duke's change of plan though it was ten years before the final scheme was started.

Robert Mylne provided the surviving design in 1780 and the plasterwork was carried out in the following two years; the ceiling with decoration cast in London by John Papworth and the cornice and frieze by the Scottish plasterer John Clayton. The ceiling plasterwork and painting were extensively restored in 2009.

'QUALITY UNPARALLELED IN BRITAIN'

The elaborate painting was completed in 1784 by two French painters Girard and Guinand, whose work only survives at Inveraray. It is of a quality unparalleled in Britain at that time and it is of little surprise to find that Girard was one of the principal decorative artists employed by the young Prince of Wales at Carlton House. Guinand, who died at Inveraray in 1784, evidently painted the grisaille roundels of the Seasons over the doors and the ovals in the main panels; Girard's painting of the garlands of flowers over the pier glasses and details such as the owls and squirrels in the narrow uprights are brilliantly done.

On the ceiling it is difficult to tell at a glance which ornaments of the central circle are raised and which are painted flat. Almost all the ornamental painting is original but the areas of plain colour were repainted in 2009. The chairs are part of a large set in the French style consisting of a pair of settees, bergères (chairs with filled-in arms), fauteuils (chairs with open arms) and side chairs, all with original Beauvais tapestry upholstery, probably ordered by the 5th Duke on one of his visits to France. Despite their French appearance the chairs were made in the Castle by two Edinburgh craftsmen called Traill in about 1782, working from a pattern chair that could have been a French original. Their gilding was also done in situ, by a French gilder called Dupasquier who first appeared in 1771 and who signed one of the chairs with the date 1782. The tapestry was apparently put on by the local tailor and he also made curtains and liveries, such as the House of Argyll livery worn by the footmen.

'DESPITE THEIR FRENCH APPEARANCE, THE CHAIRS WERE MADE IN THE CASTLE'

THE SPECTACULAR AND INTRICATE SILVER GILT SHIP TABLE DECORATIONS ARE CALLED 'NEFS'. GERMAN IN MANUFACTURE, THEY DATE FROM THE 19TH CENTURY. IF YOU LOOK CLOSELY, YOU WILL SEE THE ARGYLL ARMS ENGRAVED IN THE SAILS

The decorated mosaic tops on the corner console tables are late 18th century Italian. The picture over the fireplace is that of the 4th Duke of Argyll in his Coronation Robes after Thomas Gainsborough

The Dining Room is very much in use today by the family for more formal occasions, corporate events and private parties, and is laid out with the china and silverware bearing the Argyll arms

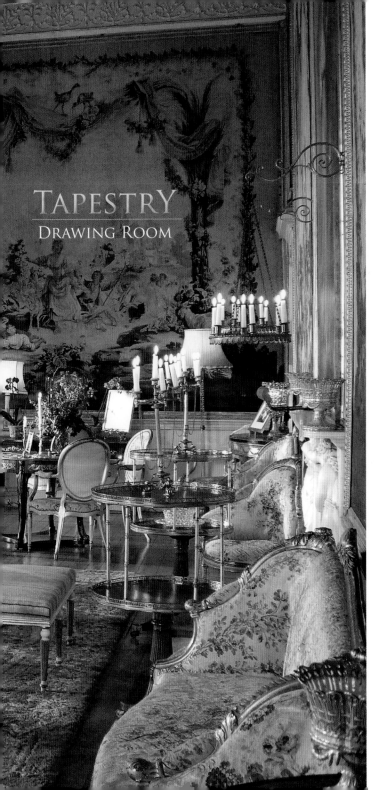

TAPESTRY
DRAWING ROOM

This room, like the Dining Room, represents the most sophisticated taste of the 1780s and it is extraordinary to think that this colourful Parisian room should have been achieved in such a remote place and that 200 years later it should still retain the original set of Beauvais tapestries in the setting specially designed for it. The architectural decoration and plasterwork were complete by the end of 1782 and the decorative painting, by Girard working on his own, was carried out between 1785 and 1788. His painting of the shutters with its thin glazes, flickering brushwork and heightening in gold is particularly brilliant. The gilding of the ceiling was probably by Dupasquier and although from the ground it appears to be done in two different colours of gold, it is one colour but with a limited use of red glaze.

> *'It is extraordinary to think that this colourful Parisian room should have been achieved in such a remote place'*

British patrons in the 1770s and 1780s had a great liking for French tapestry, and the Inveraray set commissioned by the 5th Duke in 1785, was hung in 1787. Known as ***Pastorales draperies bleues et arabesques***, after J. B. Huet, it is thought to be the only set of 18th century Beauvais tapestries still in the room for which it was made. Panels to go over the doors were not supplied and so overdoors had to be painted, presumably by Girard. The tapestries were cleaned and restored by the Textile Conservation Centre at Hampton Court Palace in 1976.

A detail from 'Pastorales draperies bleues et arabesques'

The pair of confidantes and the set of matching armchairs, together with the two white and gilt armchairs, were supplied to the 5th Duke by John Linnell in about 1775, and the other set of six chairs in the French Hepplewhite style are of the same period. The fact that the confidantes were ordered before the tapestries might explain the slightly awkward line of their backs against the base of the tapestries

The circular giltwood palm tree table with its specimen marble top is inlaid with the arms of the 7th Duke and his third wife, Anne Colquhoun Cuninghame of Craigends, whom he married in 1831. The mantelpiece was installed in 1800. The panel of dancing girls is by George Richmond, painted about 1846

Robert Adam's original drawing for the ceiling

Aurora

Lady Charlotte Campbell

by John Hoppner

*Here pictured as the Roman goddess of dawn,
from whom the aurora borealis gets its name,
Lady Charlotte Campbell (1775 - 1861) was more
famously known as the popular writer and diarist,
Lady Bury. Daughter of the 5th Duke & Duchess,
she was renowned for her beauty.
A leading light in Georgian Society she became a
lady-in-waiting to Queen Caroline and produced
a celebrated Diary of the goings-on of the Court of
George IV (earlier, the Prince Regent)*

The entrance to the Turret is ingeniously concealed by a pair of double doors in the corner of the Drawing Room which are covered with tapestry as part of the panels. The papier-mâché ceiling was designed by Mylne in 1773.

The display cabinets in this room contain a collection of Oriental and European porcelain, including Japanese Imari-ware of the early 18th century, in its typical palette of underglaze blue, iron-red and gilding, Chinese blue and white, a Meissen dessert service, a combined Meissen and replacement Chamberlain's Worcester service, a large Derby dinner service of the early 19th century and other pieces of English porcelain.

CHINA
TURRET

A Barr porcelain cabinet cup decorated after a Sèvres original

ARMOURY
HALL

*Robert The Bruce,
sculpted by Princess
Louise, Queen Victoria's
daughter and wife of
the 9th Duke (see the
Victorian Room)*

The dramatic concept of linking the Central Hall to the twin flanking staircases was derived from Vanbrugh's entrance halls at Castle Howard and Blenheim, but here the effect of soaring height (21 metres) and generous open spaces is made more exciting by the fall of light from different directions through the arches.

The idea of displays of arms in decorative patterns also dates back to Vanbrugh's period, but the present arrangement is an elaboration of that ordered by the 5th Duke in 1783. The display includes a collection of 16th and 17th century pole-arms and roundels of Brown Bess muskets dating from around 1740 with spandrels of muskets alternated with Lochaber axes, the latter from the time of Queen Victoria's first visit to Inveraray in 1847, and 18th century Scottish broadswords. The impressive bronze of Robert the Bruce on horseback was sculpted by Princess Louise; a remarkably talented woman.

Busts of the Marquess of Lorne and Lady Edith Campbell with the painted Argyll Arms on the ceiling

THE DISPLAY TABLES CONTAIN A FASCINATING COLLECTION
OF ITEMS AND TREASURES ASSOCIATED WITH INVERARAY, THE
LONG HISTORY OF THE CAMPBELL CLAN AND FAMILY AND
OTHER HIGHLAND OBJECTS OF INTEREST.

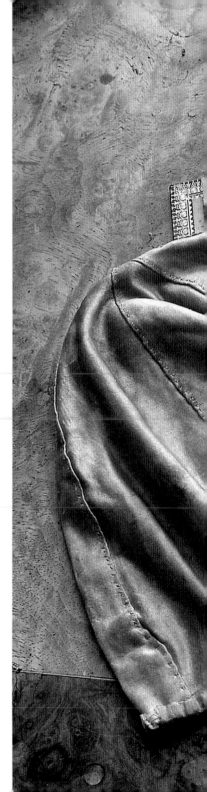

Above:
Highland dirks & plaid brooch

Right: Rob Roy's belt & sporran

Below:
The wedding quaich for Sir John
Campbell of Glenorchy and Mary
Campbell, daughter of the Earl of
Argyll in 1678, with a decorative
gunpowder flask created from an
animal horn

Right: The speech
of the Marquess of
Argyll, made before
his execution in 1661,
with his skull cap and a
miniature

The piano here has a remarkable history all of its own. It was on its keys that American musical duo, Lerner & Loewe, composed several of the songs for 'My Fair Lady'. Audrey Hepburn's interpretation of Eliza Doolittle made the 1964 film version unforgettable

Either side of the two large portraits are gilded appliqués from 1788: to reflect the Saloon's use as a place to play music, their design is influenced by a harp

SALOON

In large 18th century houses the Saloon was usually the most formal room for the reception of guests, but it seems that from the beginning, the 5th Duke envisaged his Saloon as a remarkably modern living room, where guests could have breakfast, read the papers, make music or play billiards. In the early 1780s the walls were hung with green damask and the main display of family portraits was arranged here with the frames of the large portraits at either end made to match the flanking appliqués.

Continuing the theme of family portraits, the piano always displays a collection of informal and treasured photographs of the immediate Argyll family. In the room is also a display of silver, including the silver-gilt dressing table set of HRH Princess Louise, Queen Victoria & Prince Albert's 4th daughter, who married the Marquess of Lorne (later 9th Duke) in 1871

The large tapestry-covered sofa and chairs are the surviving pieces of a much larger set produced in 1782

Also notice how the large Gainsborough portrait was increased in size to match the Batoni picture on the opposite facing wall

Unfortunately by 1950, the damask was so decayed that it had to be taken down but the walls have recently been repainted from the original background colour of the cornice. The room is used today for a variety of functions, where guests are watched over by the portraits of Dukes, Duchesses and children of the family.

1ST DUKE
ARCHIBALD

*In Roman costume
with his two sons,
John, later 2nd Duke
and Archibald,
3rd Duke by Sir
John Medina*

2ND DUKE
JOHN

*In Garter robes
by Allan Ramsay
dated 1740*

Opposite left: The 5th Duke in armour by Cosway and his four children by his wife, Elizabeth Gunning, Duchess of Hamilton, by William Opie

Field Marshal the Rt. Hon. Henry Seymour-Conway, son-in-law of the 4th Duke of Argyll by Gainsborough

Jane Warburton, wife of John, 2nd Duke of Argyll by Aikman

FURTHER
SALOON
PORTRAITS

Captain Lord William Campbell RN, Governor of Novia Scotia (1766) and of South Carolina (1773). Brother of the 5th Duke. By Francis Cotes

Lord Frederick Campbell, 3rd son of the 4th Duke of Argyll. Lord Clerk Register of Scotland by Edinburgh artist, George Willison

John, 2nd Duke of Argyll and Greenwich by Aikman

The 8th Duke of Hamilton by Pompeo Batoni.

Son of Elizabeth Gunning (see the Staircase), wife of the 5th Duke of Argyll, by her previous marriage to the 6th Duke of Hamilton.

Based in Rome, Batoni made a career out of painting flamboyant 'swagger' portraits of mainly British nobleman on their 'Grand Tours' of the Continent. Quite a holiday souvenir ...

Alice, Countess of Drogheda by Sir Peter Lely

Mary, Countess of Dalhousie by Wissing, later Lady Bellenden

IAN,
12TH DUKE
OF ARGYLL
(1937-2001)

NORTH WEST HALL
&
STAIRCASE

The North West Hall & Staircase leads the way to the upper floor. Notice the Brussels tapestry and enjoy the fascinating Bronze & Iron Age antiquities in the cabinets, including swords and an unusually large ceremonial axe-head.

The background photograph here features two of the Highland swords on display

MARY GUNNING
COUNTESS OF COVENTRY
(1732-1760)
BY KATHERINE READ

ARCHIBALD, EARL OF
ISLAY AFTERWARDS
3RD DUKE OF ARGYLL
(1682-1761)
BY ALLAN
RAMSAY

ARCHIBALD, 9TH EARL
OF ARGYLL, WHEN LORD
LORNE
(1629- BEHEADED 1685)
BY MARY BEALE

LADY MARGARET DOUGLAS
WIFE OF ARCHIBALD,
8TH EARL & MARQUESS
OF ARGYLL
(1610-1678)
BY J.SUSTERMANS

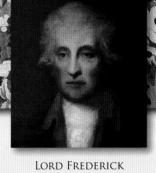

LORD FREDERICK
CAMPBELL
BROTHER OF THE 5TH
DUKE OF ARGYLL &
LORD CLERK REGISTRAR
BY GAINSBOROUGH
DUPONT

GEORGE, 6TH DUKE
OF ARGYLL (1768-1839)
LORD STEWARD IN
QUEEN VICTORIA'S FIRST
MINISTRY
BY SIR HENRY RAEBURN

ELIZABETH GUNNING,
DUCHESS OF ARGYLL
(1733-1790)
BY KATHERINE READ

JOHN, 7TH DUKE OF ARGYLL (1777-1847)
BY SIR HENRY RAEBURN

JOHN, 5TH DUKE OF
ARGYLL (1723-1806)
BY THOMAS
GAINSBOROUGH

IN THE HALL & UP THE STAIRCASE IS A SERIES OF PORTRAITS
OF MEMBERS OF THE ARGYLL FAMILY. THE STAIRCASE LEADS TO
THE DISPLAY OF ROBES AND ON TO THE FIRST FLOOR ROOMS.

ARCHIBALD, 3RD DUKE
OF ARGYLL (1682-1761)
AS LORD JUSTICE-
GENERAL BY ALLAN
RAMSAY

SIR JAMES CAMPBELL OF
ARDKINGLAS
BY WILLIAM AIKMAN

ROBES WORN AT THE CORONATION OF KING EDWARD VII IN 1902. THE SMALLER CORONET WAS LAST WORN BY PRINCESS MARINA OF KENT AT THE CORONATION OF QUEEN ELIZABETH II IN 1953.

POMP
&
CIRCUMSTANCE

The stunning and intricate gold embroidery of Duchess Louise's Coronation Dress of 1902

Robes and regalia are very much part of the unique and colourful traditions of the British aristocracy when attending State and official occasions. In the display cabinet half way up the staircase is a collection of those worn by the Dukes & Duchesses of Argyll with the present Duchess's silk wedding gown by Bruce Oldfield, taking centre stage. Also here are the robes of the Order of the Thistle (below centre) and 18th century Argyll household banners (below right). The velvet covered baton topped with the seated Crowned lion, the Scottish Royal Crest, is used by the Hereditary Master of the Royal Household in Scotland and is carried by the Duke of Argyll on ceremonial occasions.

The decorative scheme of arms is continued from the Armoury Hall up the floors to the ceiling, where the painted shields of other branches of the family can be seen

Ian Douglas, 11th Duke of Argyll (1903-1973) by Cowan Dobson

GALLERY
PORTRAITS

Archibald, 7th Earl of Argyll (1575-1638)

Above centre: Niall, later 10th Duke (1872-1949) by Sir William Blake Richmond

Above: John, 9th Duke (1845-1914)

Below: John, 4th Duke (1693-1770)

Duchess of Sutherland by Winterhalter. Her daughter married the 8th Duke of Argyll

King George III
(1738-1820).
Both this and the
matching portrait of the
Queen (below) bear the
inscription:

Presented to
The Duchess of Argyll
Mistress of The Robes
by Queen Charlotte.
After Zoffany

John, 7th Duke of Argyll
(1777-1847) by H.P. Briggs

Portrayed at the front
entrance of the Castle, notice
the distinctive stonework
below and Dun na Cuaiche
rising beyond in the
background

His wife :
Queen Charlotte
(1744-1818).
A keen amateur botanist,
she was instrumental in
the foundation of
Kew Gardens.
The King and Queen
produced 15 children

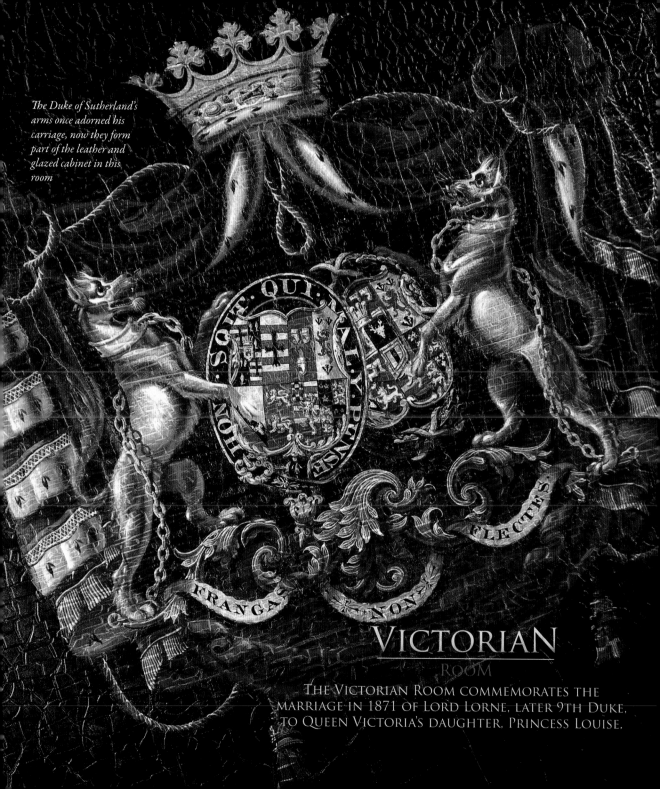

The Duke of Sutherland's arms once adorned his carriage, now they form part of the leather and glazed cabinet in this room

SOIT · QUI · MAL · Y · PENSE · HONI

FRANGAS · NON · FLECTES

VICTORIAN
ROOM

THE VICTORIAN ROOM COMMEMORATES THE MARRIAGE IN 1871 OF LORD LORNE, LATER 9TH DUKE, TO QUEEN VICTORIA'S DAUGHTER, PRINCESS LOUISE.

Princess Louise by Koberwein after Winterhalter

The Marquess of Lorne by Barclay

Detail from Sydney Hall's painting of the wedding. See over the page

The 8th Duke of Argyll by Baron Heinrich von Angeli

MANY ITEMS ON DISPLAY ARE REMINDERS OF THE OCCASION, PRINCIPALLY THE MAPLEWOOD WRITING DESK, GIVEN BY THE QUEEN TO HER DAUGHTER AS A WEDDING GIFT.

Below: Princess Louise's writing desk

Pâte-sur-pâte vase by M.L. Solon with portrait medallions of the Bride and Groom. It was commissioned as a gift by Colin Campbell Minton

Below right: Queen Victoria at her spinning wheel accompanied by a favourite dog. A biscuit-ware figure by Princess Louise, an accomplished sculptor

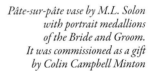

MARRIAGE OF
LORD LORNE TO PRINCESS LOUISE
1871

(St George's Chapel, Windsor)

PAINTED FOR LORD LORNE BY SYDNEY HALL ESQ.

Standing behind Queen Victoria is
HRH The Prince of Wales,
later King Edward VII -
Princess Louise's eldest brother

The Bride:
Princess Louise,
4th daughter of
Queen Victoria
& the late Prince Albert

HRH Princess Beatrice,
one of The Bride's
sisters, and namesake
of the present Duke of
York's elder daughter

HRH The Princess of
Wales, later Queen
Alexandra with her two
sons, (left) HRH Prince
George, the future King
George V, and (right)
HRH Prince Albert Victor

Among the honoured guests was Duleep Singh (wearing the turban), former Maharajah of Lahore, India. Deposed in 1849, aged only 11, he was brought to England where he was unofficially adopted by The Queen and Prince Albert, holidaying with the Royal family at Osborne House, Isle of Wight. As an adult, his fondness for partying became legendary, and he is pictured here at the height of his social popularity before financial difficulties led him to leave the country. After spending some time in Russia, he moved to Paris where he died alone and in poverty in 1893. Standing to his left is his first wife, Bamba Miller, a former missionary. Their eldest son, Prince Victor Albert Jay Duleep Singh, was named in honour of Queen Victoria and Prince Albert, and grew up to marry the youngest daughter of the Earl of Coventry. A fascinating character, Duleep's life is the subject of a book by Peter Bance *Sovereign, Squire & Rebel*. He even has his own website: www.duleepsingh.com

The Groom:
John, Marquess of Lorne, later 9th Duke of Argyll

Parents of The Groom: George 8th Duke & Duchess Elizabeth of Argyll. (The Duke's attire can be seen in full detail in his portrait left of the fireplace)

Prime Minister
William Gladstone

Future Prime Minister,
Lord Beaconsfield
(better known as
Benjamin Disraeli)

THE 'DOUBLE DUCHESS'
ELIZABETH GUNNING,
WIFE OF 5TH DUKE

THE SINGING YOUTH:
NOT A POPULAR
PICTURE

MACARTHUR
ROOM

Ghost hunters will detect a distinct chill in the air in this room. The hauntings centre around the elaborately carved bed on which a young Irish harpist was murdered in 1644. Legend has it that the boy's ghost became so attached to the bed that when it was moved to the present castle, his spirit came too. When a member of the family is about to die, it is said that harp music is heard coming from this room. The last report of this supernatural phenomenon being in 1949, when the 10th Duke died. However, a recent recording of the television show 'Most Haunted' (October 2009) showed the little tapestry chair and the bed moving across the room, and a number of Guides and visitors comment on the strange atmosphere there. Other ghostly apparitions at Inveraray include: The Grey Lady, who can allegedly only be seen by daughters of a Duke of Argyll, and The Galley of Lorne, a boat seen on the horizon, floating away from the Castle following the death of a Duke.

The bed - traditionally the State bed of the MacArthurs of Loch Awe - is hung with Campbell tartan. It is a little known fact that the widespread use of Scottish tartan was started by King George IV and popularised by Prince Albert on his visits with Queen Victoria. Tartan had been banned in 1746 in an attempt to bring the warrior clans under control and when legal again, became the national dress of Scotland.

THE PICTURES INCLUDE SCOTTISH PORTRAITS OF ANNE NASMYTH OF POSSO AND HER TWO CHILDREN, AND ELIZABETH GUNNING, KNOWN AS THE DOUBLE DUCHESS AFTER HER MARRIAGES TO THE 6TH DUKE OF HAMILTON AND THE 5TH DUKE OF ARGYLL. THE SINGING YOUTH WAS DISLIKED BY THE 12TH DUKE WHO OFTEN TURNED IT TO FACE THE WALL. THE COLLECTION OF MINIATURES ON THE MANTLEPIECE HAVE A FAINTLY MYSTERIOUS AIR IN KEEPING WITH THE GHOSTLY ATMOSPHERE HERE.

THE TRIPLE PORTRAIT ABOVE THE FIREPLACE IS OF IAN, JAMES AND PATRICK CAMPBELL OF ARDKINGLAS, BY GEORGE JAMESTONE

The window of the MacArthur Room affords an excellent view of the Gardens, while the adjoining Turret contains a gallery of Argyll family photographs & memorabilia

THE DUKE IS PICTURED IN HIS ROLE AS
THE HEREDITARY MASTER OF THE
ROYAL HOUSEHOLD IN SCOTLAND
WITH THE CEREMONIAL SWORD
AND THE BATON TOPPED WITH THE
SEATED CROWNED LION,
THE SCOTTISH ROYAL CREST

BY ROYAL APPOINTMENT

THE STATE OPENING OF PARLIAMENT ATTENDED BY
THEIR ROYAL HIGHNESSES, THE PRINCE & PRINCESS OF
WALES. ON THE RIGHT BEHIND THE ROYAL COUPLE,
IS THE PRESENT DUKE (THEN MARQUESS OF LORNE)
IN HIS ROLE AS PAGE OF HONOUR TO HER MAJESTY.

*Certificate from The Lord Chamberlain's Office, dated January 1st 1981, appointing the present Duke to the role of Page of Honour to HM The Queen.
He was aged 12 at the time*

'To have, hold, exercise and enjoy the said Place, together with all Rights, Profits, Privileges and Advantages thereunto belonging'

On behalf of all concerned in the advancement, standing and reputation of Scotch whisky we hereby admit His Grace The Duke of Argyll to the roll of

THE KEEPERS OF THE QUAICH

in the presence of the Grand Master Ian Good
on this day October 3 · 2005 at Blair Castle, Blair Atholl
in the county of Perthshire, Scotland

Chairman *Richard Worning*   Secretary *The Calthould*

Roll No. 1566   Life Member

UISGEBEATHA GU BRATH

'THE WATER OF LIFE - FOREVER'

'The Keepers of the Quaich is a Society at the heart of the Scotch Whisky industry. It was founded by the main companies in the industry with the purpose of promoting the heritage and quality of Scotch Whisky on an international level through its members in 83 countries'

The Duke was admitted to the Society in 2005 and was made a Patron in 2008. Here he holds 'The Quaich', the ancient ceremonial drinking vessel.

In his work for Chivas Brothers, the Duke attends a variety of promotional events; here with Hollywood actress Julianne Moore at the Chivas Regal party, New York Public Library, Sept 2007, launching a 25yr old blend. The actress was accepting bottle No.1 on behalf of New York City. Her mother was born in Dunoon

Photo: Richard Young

Surprisingly, the game is faster than one would expect, with extremely skilled stick and ball work (the sticks are made of bamboo and can range from 6 to 9 feet) and the elephant can often become more excited than the players. Most games have an incident which includes elephants running away with sticks, treading on balls (which can take minutes to dig out) and generally taking the game over amongst themselves. The rules have some necessary additions which include a penalty for elephants lying down over the goal and wandering off to eat bamboo shoots - none of which is helped by the fact that elephants don't understand English!

TROPHIES
TRUNKS

In 2004 and 2005 the Duke of Argyll captained his team, Chivas Regal Scotland, to win the World Elephant Polo Championships in Nepal and the King's Cup in Thailand, making a unique double.

The World Elephant Polo Association (WEPA) was formed in 1982 at Tiger Tops, Nepal, and has an enormous and growing following of fans and teams from all over the world. The Duke represents Scotland and competes twice a year against teams from Hong Kong, India, Iceland, Thailand, England, Nepal, Germany, USA, Australia and Sri Lanka to name but a few.

'THERE IS USUALLY A GIANT ELEPHANT
USED FOR REFEREEING'

The rules of the game are similar to horse polo, although played at a much slower pace with four elephants on each side. Each elephant is 'driven' by an expert Mahout, which leaves the player to concentrate on the game (as well as trying to stay on the animal!). The smaller elephants are used for the attack positions as they are generally faster, while the slower and larger elephants are used to block and defend the goal. There is usually a giant elephant used for refereeing and a number of vital helpers including the umpires, commentators and of course, the 'official pooper scoopers'.

'NONE OF WHICH IS HELPED BY THE FACT
THAT ELEPHANTS DON'T UNDERSTAND ENGLISH!'

The Duke is a key player in the main Scottish team which has been dominating the game since it started in Nepal in 1982. Scotland has a strong, even if unlikely, link with the game. It was originally played by Scots in India at the turn of the century and was started up again in 1982 by James Manclark from Edinburgh. The games - held in Thailand and Nepal - always have a 'Scottish' feel to them with the ceremonies being opened and closed with a selection of music played on the bagpipes, accompanied by the World Elephant Polo official drink - Chivas Regal Whisky.

1968: Ian and Iona at the christening of Torquhil, present Duke, with grandparents, Ian, 11th Duke and Duchess Louise in the Castle doorway. The other children don't seem too impressed though

1974: Ian, 12th Duke & Duchess Iona dancing the night away at the Washington St Andrews Society Ball

HAPPY
DAYS

August 2004: Proud parents and grandmother - the Duke & Duchess with Iona Dowager Duchess, at the christening of Archie Frederick, Marquess of Lorne

*Torquhil & Eleanor
13th Duke & Duchess of Argyll*

Official engagement photograph 2002

WEDDING
BELLE

Escorted by her father Peter Cadbury, Eleanor wore a dress of ivory silk by Bruce Oldfield, which can be seen alongside other notable Argyll family clothes and formal robes half way up the Castle staircase

THE DUKE OF ARGYLL
MARRIES HIS CADBURY ROSE

'Two famous British dynasties came together when the Duke of Argyll married his long-time sweetheart Eleanor Cadbury in a romantic ceremony in Gloucestershire. The chieftain of Clan Campbell proposed to Eleanor on the summit of Table Mountain in Cape Town

As part of the day's celebrations, the couple took a romantic punt down the petal-strewn Thames'

Photos: Clive Postlethwaite / Hello Magazine
Words: Hello Magazine

1921: Niall, 10th Duke with his cousin Ian Douglas Campbell, later 11th Duke, enjoying the Inveraray Highland Games

1950: The 11th Duke & Duchess with Ian, Marquess of Lorne, later 12th Duke, at the Argyllshire Gathering

1964: Sir Ivar & Lady Colquhoun, the 12th Duke's parents-in-law, with the 11th Duke & Duchess at the wedding of the Marquess of Lorne to Iona, their daughter

1966: The 11th Duke accepting the 8th Battalion Argyll & Sutherland Highlander's Regimental Colours, from Brigadier Lorne Campbell VC, DSO, TD, at the front porch of the Castle. How times have changed - the event is covered by a journalist with a 16mm 'film' camera

NE OBLIVISCARIS

'LEST WE FORGET'

IAN 12TH DUKE OF ARGYLL

1,000 say farewell to Duke of Argyll

'We remember him for his friendship and kindness, his great sense of loyalty and public duty'

Rev Brian Wilkinson

AN HONOUR GUARD OF THE ARGYLL AND SUTHERLAND HIGHLANDERS
BEAR THE DUKE'S COFFIN AS FAMILY AND MOURNERS FOLLOW

Words: Jim McBeth / Photo: Donald MacLeod

IAN CAMPBELL
12TH DUKE OF ARGYLL

BORN AUGUST 28TH 1937
DIED APRIL 21ST 2001

NE · OBLIVISCARIS

EDUCATED IN SCOTLAND AND
SWITZERLAND HE WENT ON TO MCGILL
UNIVERSITY IN CANADA. IN 1953 HE WAS
MADE A FELLOW IN THE ROYAL
SOCIETY FOR THE ENCOURAGEMENT OF
THE ARTS, MANUFACTURES & COMMERCE
AND SERVED WITH THE ARGYLL AND
SUTHERLAND HIGHLANDERS,
BECOMING A CAPTAIN. HE WAS INVESTED
AS A KNIGHT IN THE ORDER OF ST. JOHN
IN 1975 AND BECAME LORD LIEUTENANT
OF ARGYLL & BUTE. MARRIED IN 1964
TO IONA COLQUHOUN, THEY HAD TWO
CHILDREN, TORQUHIL - THE PRESENT
DUKE - AND LOUISE.

HMS Argyll
launched in
1904

F231 moored in Rothesay Bay, for the occasion of the present
Duke & Duchess's daughter Charlotte's Christening, in 2009

O ne of the most exciting titles held by the
Duke of Argyll is that of Admiral of The
West & Isles and as a result, he has strong
bonds with the vessel that bears his name; HMS
Argyll. In 1715, the first 'HMS' Argyll was a 50-
gun Ship of The Line. After an interval of 160 years
the second ship to bear the name was a 10,000 ton
armoured cruiser of 1904 (above). After successful
action in WWI, she ran aground on the Bell Rock near
Dundee, due to the rock's lighthouse being switched
off to hamper German U-boats in their operations.

8th May 1995:
HMS Argyll
at Plymouth
Hoe enjoying
the VE
Day 50th
anniversary
celebrations

Photograph
presented to
the Duke &
Duchess on
their visit to the
ship in Loch
Fyne, July 1995

ADMIRAL
OF
THE WEST & ISLES

The Duke &
Duchess with
F231's two
30mm saluting
guns

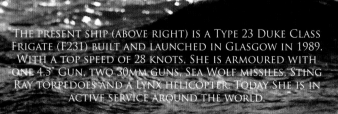

THE PRESENT SHIP (ABOVE RIGHT) IS A TYPE 23 DUKE CLASS
FRIGATE (F231) BUILT AND LAUNCHED IN GLASGOW IN 1989.
WITH A TOP SPEED OF 28 KNOTS, SHE IS ARMOURED WITH
ONE 4.5" GUN, TWO 30MM GUNS, SEA WOLF MISSILES, STING
RAY TORPEDOES AND A LYNX HELICOPTER. TODAY SHE IS IN
ACTIVE SERVICE AROUND THE WORLD.

Officers and
crew of F231
with the
Admiral of the
West & Isles, the
Duke of Argyll

Gannets off South Uist, Outer Hebrides
Photo: Nick McCann

CLAN
CAMPBELL

The Duke of Argyll is MacCailein Mor, Head of Clan Campbell, meaning 'Son of the Great Colin - the 'first' of the Campbells. Knighted in 1280 he held lands around Loch Awe. Later, the family were supporters of King Robert the Bruce, and the rest, as they say, is history. Today there are thousands of loyal Clan members all over the world, and Inveraray Castle and other venues in Scotland are hugely proud when members travel vast distances for reunions and celebrations, such as the World Reunion at Dunedin, New Zealand in 1988 (above) and the Clan Gathering at the Castle in July 2009, attended by the Duke & Duchess and their family, pictured here in the Armoury Hall.

THE OLD KITCHEN IS SITUATED OFF THE PRESENT DAY TEA ROOM LINKING THE PAST WITH THE PRESENT IN A VERY CULINARY WAY.

OLD
KITCHEN

The original Castle kitchen was last used by the Duke's grandmother, Duchess Louise, in the 1950s. It is a unique kitchen with seven fireplaces: two stewing stoves, two baking ovens, a hot plate, boiling stove and a roasting fire with working spit which would originally have been operated by a fan in the chimney. There is a fine collection of copper utensils known as *batterie de cuisine*, together with various utensils of the Victorian, Edwardian and pre-World War II eras.

batterie de cuisine

| RROW ROOT | B.k PEPPER | COCOA | | SAGO | TAPIOCCA | GROUND RI |

| P.: MACCARONI | RI.B MACCARONI | | HARTS.H SHAVINGS | | PR.E BARL |

| CURRANTS | | | SUN RAISINS |

| INGER | CLOVES & NUTMEGS | CINNAMON & MACE | SUGAR CANDY | WH.T PEPPER | JAM.A PEPP |

| O.R ALMONDS | BIT.R ALMONDS | | VERMICELLI | | ISINGLASS |

| CLAYED SUGAR | | | STARCH | and | BLUE |

ON THE WELL-WORN KITCHEN CHEST OF DRAWERS IS A POSITIVE ENCYCLOPEDIA OF INGREDIENTS GIVING A CLUE TO THE BAKING AND COOKERY THAT WOULD HAVE TAKEN PLACE IN DAYS GONE BY.

PERHAPS TODAY'S CHEFS WOULD STRUGGLE TO KNOW PRECISELY WHAT TO DO WITH ALL OF THESE, OR DETERMINE EXACTLY WHAT SOME OF THEM ARE ...

'HARTS SHAVINGS' - from the antlers of red deer stags, were a good source of ammonia and when boiled produced a gelatinous substance used in the preparation of jellies and the like

GRACE & FLAVOUR

FISHY DISHES FROM THE DUCHESS OF ARGYLL

In association with

INVERAWE
Scotlands Specialist Smokehouse

INVERAWE
Scotlands Specialist Smokehouse

www.smokedsalmon.co.uk

INVERAWE SALMON QUICHE
(MAIN PICTURE LEFT)
*This is such an easy recipe and so yummy.
It takes no time at all!*

INGREDIENTS

100g sliced Inverawe smoked salmon
6" or 7" bought in pastry cases (see, I told you it was easy!)
1 tbsp thinly sliced onion
3 beaten eggs with a little milk
5-6 dtsp of full fat cream cheese (optional)

METHOD

1. Cut the smoked salmon into strips and lay
into the pastry case.

2. Thinly slice onion and sprinkle on top.

3. Season the beaten eggs and milk then pour over
the fish and onion.

4. Dollop 5-6 knobs of full fat cream cheese over the top.

5. Finally swirl 2 tbsp of double cream over the lot
and season with black pepper.

6. Bake in the oven at 185°C for 20-30 minutes till
cooked - it should be just firm.

TO SERVE
*Serve hot or cold with new boiled potatoes, or go super healthy
and have a large green salad. Don't forget a glass of good
Sauvignon Blanc from Marlborough, New Zealand
to accompany the dish - it's a must!*

INVERAWE ROAST SMOKED
SALMON SALAD
A great winter salad

INGREDIENTS

200g Inverawe roast smoked salmon
1 raw beetroot
1 raw carrot
shredded white cabbage

10 green seedless grapes, halved
10 red seedless grapes, halved
Inverawe dressing

4 tbsp olive oil
1 tbsp fresh lemon juice
half tsp Dijon mustard
pinch of sugar
salt & freshly ground black pepper

METHOD

1. Julienne the carrots and beetroot.
2. Toss with equal amounts of white cabbage and add the grapes.
3. Drizzle over 3 tbsp of Inverawe dressing.

TO SERVE
*Serve on a bed of radicchio lettuce with the roasted salmon flaked
over. 200g should be enough for two people for a main course.*

SANDW...

INVERAWE
+ CREAM
AYRSHIRE H
AYRSHIRE HA
TUNA MELT
* ALL OF THE

BAGELS

INVE
AYRS
CAKE

SCONES, FRUIT or

OLD FASHIONED
FRUIT LOAF
£1·95

CALORIE
COUNTER

Run personally by the Duchess, the Castle Tearoom offers a mouth-watering menu using the best of local and West Highland ingredients. Our Scottish-sourced menu also includes the best of Mull cheddars and ice creams from Arran, while our soups, quiches and scones are made daily in the Castle and cakes are baked by our tenant farmer's wife on the estate. We are lucky to have the world renowned Inverawe Smokehouse as a neighbour, with its smoked salmons, meats and locally caught seafood. There is a wide choice of natural fruit juices, waters and first class coffees & teas - or if you really want to treat yourself, why not try a family favourite and have a Duke's Special hot chocolate?!

SOUPS, SALADS, SMOOTHIES, SNACKS & GORGEOUS GIFTS FOR GOURMETS

HOME MADE

RETAIL THERAPY

S hop before you hop. Before you leave, come and visit the fabulous Castle Shop. With each item personally chosen by the Duke's mother, the Shop has something for everyone. We sell a unique range of Scottish gifts, clothing, jewellery, books, food, children's toys and soaps. There is much on the Clan Campbell, Scottish history and of course Inveraray and the Castle, as well as more general interest titles, maps, guides DVDs & CDs.

WHETHER IT'S SOMETHING TO REMEMBER YOUR VISIT BY, A GIFT FOR SOMEONE SPECIAL, OR A THANK YOU FOR THE NEIGHBOUR WATERING THE PLANTS BACK HOME, YOU'LL PICK UP THE PERFECT PRESENT.

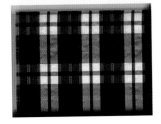

SHOP AT
INVERARAY CASTLE

GIFTS

CRAFTS

BOOKS

GAMES

CLOTHES

AND MORE

Planting
POLICIES
(The Gardens & Grounds)

The climate in Argyll, with its yearly average rainfall of 230cms (90 inches), is ideally suited to Rhododendrons and Azaleas, which flower in the gardens from April until June

Firstly, to avoid any initial confusion for those not familiar with the term, *'policies'*, is a Scots term for the improved grounds surrounding a country house. It may date back to the early 1600s. At Inveraray it is fairly certain that three of the important avenues in the area, the Lime Avenue radiating to the South West of the Castle, the Town Avenue, part of which forms the present day car park in the Town of Inveraray and the Glen Shira Avenue, date from *circa* 1650 during the lifetime of the Marquess of Argyll. A contemporary report states that the Earl of Argyll's *"dwelling pallace had sundrie zeairds (yards or gardens) some of them with divers kinds of herbs growing and sett therein-till. And other zeairds with sundrie fruit trees verie prettily sett, and planted, and there faire green lawns to walk upone, with one wall of stone builded laitlie about the said green".*

The next major phase of the development of the policies was between 1743 and 1780. During this period the 'Watch Tower' at the top of the hill to the North of the Castle, the Doocot, which can be seen from the Avenue leading from the North West of the Castle car park, and Garden or Frews Bridge, were constructed, to name three buildings. Sections of the River Aray were canalised and cascades set in place to enhance the sound of the flowing water.

As was the custom elsewhere during the latter part of the 19th century, distinguished people who visited the Castle were asked to plant trees. These included Queen Victoria, David Livingstone, William Gladstone, the Earl of Shaftesbury and others. Extending to some 180 hectares, they form one of the most important designed landscapes in Scotland and a plan is currently being developed by the Estate for their management and preservation.

In 1848 the 8th Duke commissioned William Nesfield to re-design the Castle Gardens. Nesfield obviously had talent, as he later went on to work for Sir William Hooker, Director of Kew Gardens

His plan for Inveraray's improvements is here

THE BORDERS ON EACH SIDE OF THE MAIN DRIVE, BEYOND THE LAWNS, ARE KNOWN AS THE 'FLAG-BORDERS' - THE PATHS HAVING BEEN LAID OUT IN THE SHAPE OF SCOTLAND'S NATIONAL FLAG, THE ST ANDREW'S CROSS IN THE 1870S. THESE BORDERS, OUTSTANDING IN THE SPRING WITH BEAUTIFUL PRUNUS 'UKON' AND PRUNUS SUBHIRTELLA, ARE UNDERPLANTED WITH AN INTERESTING MIXTURE OF RHODODENDRONS, EUCRYPYIAS, VARIOUS SHRUBS AND HERBACEOUS PLANTS, GIVING INTEREST ALL YEAR ROUND.

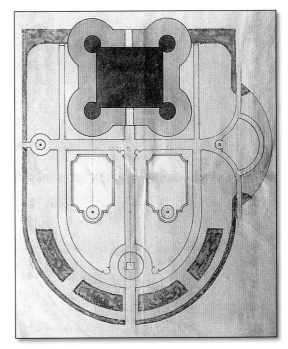

THE GARDEN COVERS SIXTEEN
ACRES, OF WHICH AROUND TWO
ACRES ARE FORMAL LAWNS AND
FLOWERBEDS, THE REMAINDER
BEING PARK AND WOODLAND.

THE GARDENS WERE OPENED
TO THE PUBLIC FOR THE FIRST
TIME IN 2010.

The 3rd Duke, who on his own admission had a 'love of laying out Grounds and Gardening' on inheriting the title and Estate in 1743, lost no time in appointing a Walter Paterson to be his gardener. He had been recruited from the 2nd Duke's staff at Caroline Park near Edinburgh and was said to be skilled in planting and 'measuring and taking levels'. It appears from his achievements that he was more of a landscape gardener than a plantsman. He was not only partly responsible for supervising the cascades in the River Aray, but created what were described as flat and featureless lawns in front of the new Castle which are seen in many of the contemporary prints.

'NAKED ON A GREEN LAWN'

In the 1820s the Castle was described by the geologist Dr John McCulloch as 'naked on a green lawn' and the Duchess of Argyll contracted a surveyor, John Brooks, to introduce some plants.

The layout of the Gardens was given its present form in the 1870s when the iron deer fence was erected, the alignment set out on the adjacent Lime Avenue and the two lawns laid in front of the Castle. Two circular and two Saltire (St Andrews Cross) flowerbeds were established. The former are now rose gardens and the latter contain a fine range of interesting shrubs.

Conifers also grow well in the poor acidic soil of a high rainfall area, as can be seen by the fine specimens such as:

Cedrus Deodars

Sequoiadendron Wellingtonia

Cryptomeria Japonica

Taxus Baccata

WINTER WONDERLAND

WALK UP TO
DUN NA CUAICHE

DUN NA CUAICHE (PRONOUNCED "DUN E QUAKE"),
RISES TO 813 FT (248M) ABOVE THE CASTLE AND LOCH
FYNE. THE NAME MEANS 'THE HILL OF THE CUP, BOWL
OR QUAICH', PROBABLY DUE TO THE HOLLOWED OUT
SHAPE OF THE SUMMIT. AT ITS SUMMIT IS AN 18TH
CENTURY 'GOTHICK' FOLLY WATCHTOWER
(OR WATERTOWER), DESIGNED BY ARCHITECT
ROGER MORRIS AND DATING FROM 1748,
IT COST £46 TO BUILD.

ITS PURPOSE WAS PURELY DECORATIVE AND IT IS
CLEVERLY SITED ON THE EDGE OF A STEEP SLOPE SO
THAT WHEN SEEN FROM THE CASTLE OR TOWN IT IS
DRAMATICALLY SILHOUETTED AGAINST THE SKY.

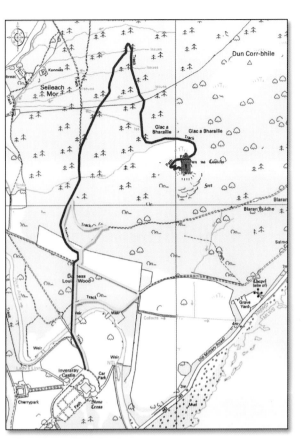

There are two walks to Dun na Cuaiche which begin from the Castle car park. The Short Walk of approximately one mile (yellow route), takes an hour or so, round trip and does not go to the summit.

The Long Walk of approximately three miles (blue route), takes you to the summit and back in around two hours. It has spectacular views of the Castle and Grounds, the town and Loch Fyne. The route to the summit is short but steep and cuts through dense woodland where, with patience, one can see a variety of native bird, animal and plant life. Stout footwear and waterproof clothing is essential.

The Miller's Lynn was built in 1802 and was used to view the waterfall and salmon leaping. It was used by Queen Victoria as a teahouse

The Doocot (Dovecote), marks the end of the former 'Oak Walk', which followed a straight line from the old castle. Doocots were common on large Scottish estates, where young doves and pigeons were reared for the table

View of Inveraray, a Seat belonging to His Grace the Duke of Argyle.

Father & son, Thomas and Paul Sandby, produced these two beautiful drawings respectively (above & below) in 1746. They show the old Inveraray before it was moved half a mile towards the loch

To his Grace the *DUKE of ARGYLE* This Prospect of Duniquich ... *INVERARAY* from the ... Grace's ...

All was peaceful at Inveraray, but at the beginning of the 1750s all that was about to change...

BELOW:

OLD INVERARAY FROM THE NORTH, 1747

ON THE RIGHT CAN BE SEEN THE OLD CASTLE AND
THE BRIDGE LEADING TO THE TOWN. IN THE CENTRE
IS THE RIVER ARAY AND TO THE LEFT, LOCH FYNE.
AT THE FAR LEFT IS 'GALLOWS FORELAND POINT',
THE SITE OF THE NEW TOWN, VIRTUALLY
UNCHANGED TODAY.

Courtesy of The British Library

A WIDER PICTURE
OF INVERARAY

Inveraray today is very much the product of one
man; Archibald, 3rd Duke of Argyll. He decided to
completely redevelop the town including 'moving it'
closer to the Loch; an 18th century case of "*Relocation,
Relocation, Relocation*".

He was naturally excited about his *Grand Conception*,
but not everyone was. One of the many families who had
to reluctantly leave their homes and businesses, left a
reminder which can be still seen today:

*In the old boundary wall -
part of which is still visible
beside the main A83 road -
the MacCorquodale family
built in a large pot and pan,
marking the spot where their
Inn used to be*

"I intend if possible to remove the town of Inveraray about half a mile lower down the Loch..."

- 3rd Duke of Argyll writing to his friend and mentor, Lord Milton, Lord Justice Clerk in 1743

The site chosen for the new town was the headland known as Ardrainach or Fern Point to the east of the avenue which today forms the main car park and which was planted by the Marquis of Argyll around 1650. The original sketch plans were made in 1744 by the 3rd Duke and the first building started in 1751 was the Argyll Hotel followed by the Town House in 1755 - where the Tourist Information Centre is now. Following the death of the 3rd Duke in 1761 and a period of inactivity during the reign of the 4th Duke, rebuilding was recommenced by the 5th Duke in 1770. He employed Robert Mylne to finalise details of the town layout and more significantly the design of the Screen Wall which forms the impressive northern facade of Inveraray

The houses and shops on either side of Main Street were built in the 1760s along with the tenements of Arkland and Relief Land. The last main building to be erected in the town to designs by Mylne was the Parish Church originally to accommodate two congregations; one Gaelic speaking and the other English speaking. Work continued on into the 19th century with the Court House, now the visitor attraction Inveraray Jail and the old School, now the Community Hall

There were few significant changes to the town for the next 150 years. In 1941 during the Second World War the church spire which had been an important focal point in the completed designs had to be removed as it had become dangerous and on account of hostilities there were insufficient resources to effect the necessary repairs. In 1956 the ownership of the Town was made over to the then Ministry of Works bringing to an end a period of some 200 years of control by the Argyll family.

Today Inveraray depends primarily on tourism for its income and attracts visitors from all over the world who come to savour the unspoilt architecture, fabulous scenery and warm hospitality. There are charming guest houses, beautiful hotels and restaurants offering the best of Argyll produce and of course the world-renowned seafood of this part of the world. A visitor in 1785 wrote:

"A commodious, elegant plan, becoming the dignity of the Capital of Argyllshire, a country most admirably suited for fisheries and navigation. The Town hath been rebuilt agreeable to the original design. The inhabitants are well lodged in houses of stone, lime and slate. They are fully employed in arts and manufactures."

www.inveraray-castle.com

"Haste ye back"

*Inveraray in 1758
by Augustino Brunias*

*Although somewhat
overly romanticised and
not particularly accurate,
geographically, it gives us an
impression of how rural and
idyllic the place was in those
early days, when the new Castle
had just been built and the New
Town was in its infancy*

*This recent aerial photograph
demonstrates how little has
really altered and one can easily
imagine how remarkable the
Castle would have appeared to
visitors in the 18th and early
19th centuries, arriving either
overland, or by ship*

Today, Inveraray may not be on a main motorway or railway route, but that of course is why it remains so unspoilt; visitors have to make the effort to reach here.

One of the more exciting ways to arrive at Inveraray will be by seaplane, operated by Loch Lomond Seaplanes - www.lochlomondseaplanes.com - Europe's premier Seaplane airline. Their aircraft will be able to fly visitors from destinations all over Scotland and further afield direct to a jetty near the Castle. See over the page in our Corporate facilities for more details, or visit our website. Here the aircraft is shown at Kilchurn Castle on Loch Awe - one of the many ancient Campbell strongholds throughout Argyll.

www.inveraray-castle.com

ROYAL SALUTE

www.inveraray-castle.com

Ronnie Cairns Wedding Photography

CORPORATE *Affairs*

I nveraray Castle is the perfect location or backdrop for weddings, private dinners, special tour groups, product launches, film and television sets, fashion shoots, concerts, meetings or car rallies.

Events can be held in the castle and gardens or in conjunction with marquees located around the castle. We have worked with the leading caterers, florists, photographers, stylists and party planners in Scotland and Great Britain to ensure that we can meet the requests of most customers. And, getting to us has never been so much fun - by seaplane, helicopter, boat or road. For further information on Inveraray Castle, contact:

The Castle Manager
Inveraray Castle
Inveraray
Argyll
PA32 8XF
Tel: 01499 302551

www.lochlomondseaplanes.com

email: manager@inveraray-castle.com

Design and photography by Nick McCann.

Additional pictures by Peter Smith and The Duke & Duchess of Argyll. Single photographs have been credited individually.

Copyright of the photographs is held by the individual photographers/copyright holders,
Inveraray Castle and Heritage House Media Ltd where appropriate.
Editorial by Nick McCann & Sarah Davison.
The publishers are grateful to the important contributions of previous authors of previous guidebooks to Inveraray,
most notably Robert Innes-Smith, George Hughes-Hartman and Alistair Campbell of Airds.

Whilst every effort has been made to trace the owners of the copyright material
reproduced herein, Inveraray Castle and the publishers would like to apologise
for any omissions and will be pleased to incorporate any missing
acknowledgements in future editions.

Produced and published by Heritage House Group
Ketteringham Hall, Wymondham
Norfolk NR18 9RS
www.hhgroup.co.uk

91764-01/10

Every effort has been made to ensure the information is correct
at the time of going to press. Inveraray Castle or Heritage House Media Ltd cannot however accept any
responsibility for any loss or damage arising from any errors or omissions.

Any image requests should be submitted to Heritage House Group or Inveraray Castle.

ISBN 978-0-85101-462-3

INVERARAY CASTLE
INVERARAY
ARGYLL
PA32 8XE

Telephone: 01499 302203
Fax: 01499 302421
email: enquiries@inveraray-castle.com

www.inveraray-castle.com